Amelie and the Bumblebee

Written by
Melinda Reynolds

Illustrated by
Robin Gulack

Enjoy Reading! Melinda Reynolds

this book belongs to: _____

To order additional copies of this book, contact:
Xlibris Corporation
1-888-795-4274
www.Xlibris.com
Orders@Xlibris.com

How to Pronounce Amelie

To pronounce Amelie correctly, open your mouth wide and say:

Ahh...
Then say Ma,
then Lee.
There, you have it!
Ah...ma...lee.
AMELIE

5

Prologue

Because Amelie lives in the city of Spokane, she loves to visit her Nanee and Papa who live on Half Moon Prairie in the country north of Spokane. Nanee and Papa have two cuddly white Bichon Frize puppy dogs named Truman and Taylor, who are always looking for fun, and a very old silky white kitty named Habeebee, who just wants to be petted or scratched under her chin.

One warm summer morning while visiting and playing outside at Nanee and Papa's house, Amelie, followed by Truman, Taylor and Habeebee had an amazing adventure!

Amelie held a Bumblebee

Underneath an old oak Tree.

"Buzz, buzz, buzz please set me free,"

Said the bumblebee to Amelie.

Gently she reached out her hand,

placing him upon the sand,

free to fly

Special friends are oh so grand.

Differences can be such fun.

Said Amelie,
"You fly. I run.

You're the color of the sun,

good times

have just

"Buzz, buzz, buzz," said the bumblebee.

and you trust me."

"We'll be friends through eternity,"

sang the bumblebee and Amelie.

Gently she reached out her hand,

placing him upon the sand,

free to fly or free to land.

Special friends are oh so grand.

Differences can be such fun.

Said Amelie. "You fly. I run.

You're the color of the sun,

and our good times have just begun."

"Buzz, buzz, buzz," said the bumblebee.

"I trust you and you trust me."

"We'll be friends through eternity,"

Sang the bumblebee and Amelie.